WARING

Sexual talk, harm, and more.

WITH LOVE

To Eve the second woman technically in this world or in this specific multi universe.

To those that ever felt like Eve or related to her in these trying times. I'm sorry what they done to you or said about your own name and I hope they deserve their own hell back.

TABLE OF CONTENTS

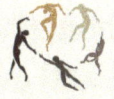

THE THIRST

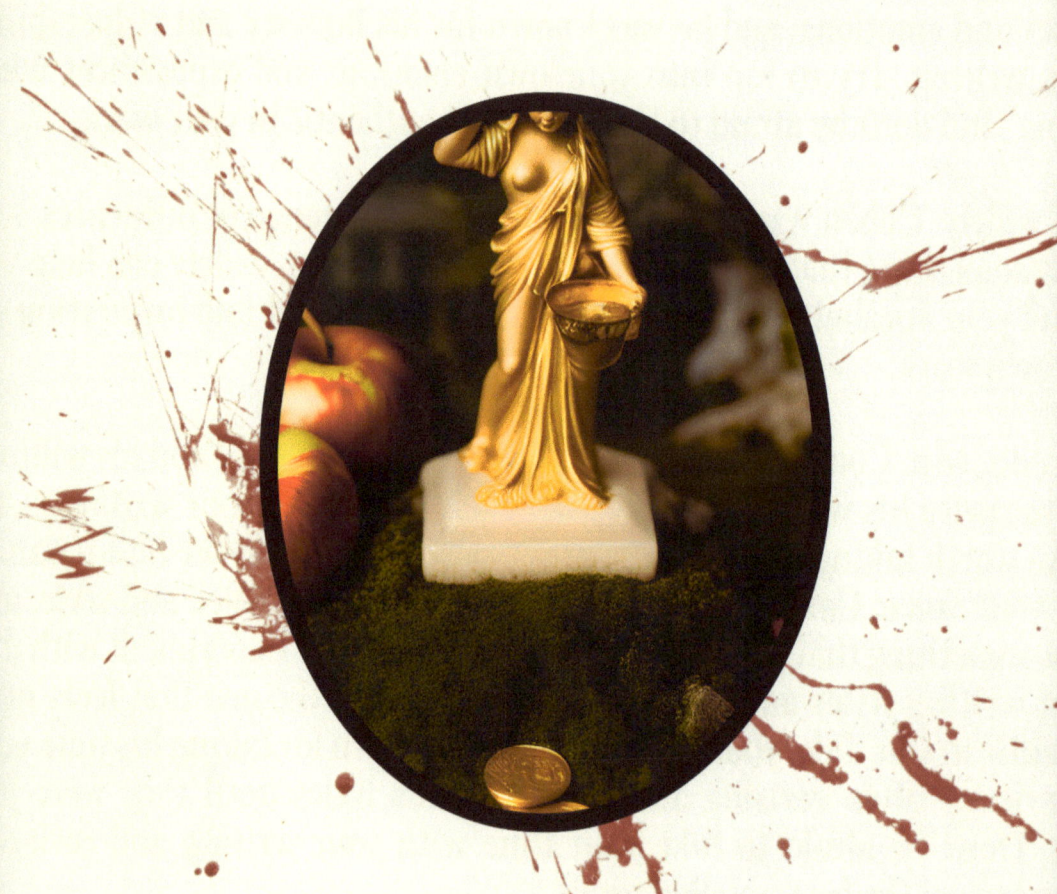

My *throat is dried*
Water can't satisfy
I *beg in prayers for knowledge and to be wise*
You can hear my cries at night

The thirst

TO THE PITS OF DESPAIR

Pushed by a force

Falling in reverse with no air

Can't stand myself as I gasped for life that once was.

What have I done?

Will God ever forgive me?

Did she, Eve ever felt just like me?

Eve was naive

But I should've known better.

Within the gardens of Eden, did she quickly

understand the fall to the dispair?

Eve tasted the forbidden fruit.

While I ripped it off knowing the wrong with a

knowing grin

And we both fell into despair so deeply

Was her heart heavy with the weight of the truth?

I wanted to know so fucking bad, now the knowledge

brought us back.

With my audacity and wisdom I will become

stronger from these pits

IN DARKNESS

In the darkness, I glow and other times I feel
alone.
You, can hear my cries?
Please deny it so.
Lost in a world that's unknown.
Will I ever be happy?
Or will I always be alone in my darkness?
Like Eve, I am searching for a way to be freed.
But together we'll found the light, I too will find
my way to what's right. Please let me happy and
safe some day. For in the darkness, there's always
hope, a chance to find a way to cope. I can heal
even if nobody else knows.
In this darkness of mine, I will grow and bloom
like moonflowers do.
Only God knows our truths, please don't let me
fall or end up blinded soon.

The thirst

LILITH IS FREE, WHAT ABOUT ME?

We watch her with a glare
We all know a Lilith in our lives
Eve felt a twinge of jealousy, as Lilith got to danced
in the moonlight free at last.
Misunderstood, she couldn't see, what Lilith did to
set herself free.
So Eve judged harshly without a knowing or care.
Yet, Lilith felt differently.
That the Lilith longed for sisterly company.
But envy blinded Eve's sight, why not me she said,
and she saw only a rival's might. Yet Lilith, with
kindness, brighter magic, and listening ears just for
her.
Still reached out to ease the spite, to treat her as her
own.
Even if she was naive, Lilith didn't try to take
advantage of Eve.
And in that moment, Eve realized, flustered that
her jealousy was unfounded and unwise. For Lilith
was not a threat in disguise, but a friend with whom
she could harmonize.

WORRIED ABOUT THE AFTERLIFE

I'm sorry, but what if hell is real, I can't risk
that.
Can't live the life I want because I'm waiting for
the afterlife to actually be happy for once.
Eve softly questioning me
We're talking about life, and my many worries
about the afterlife. What if there's nothing
beyond,no heaven, no hell, no God, and no eternal
bond?
She gets quiet with a frown.
I pondered the mysteries of death as I slowly
spiral of my eventual death.
Hey, don't do that she says.
And what happens when we take our last
breath. I know she can't answer that even if she
wants to.
But in the end, we both agreed, that living fully
is all we need. So let's cherish each moment we're
alive, making the most of our time to thrive. For
whether there's an afterlife or not, our legacy on
Earth will be our lasting plot. I chose my mental
health first for once in my life.

SHAMED INTO RESPONSIBILITY

Eve *nicely listens to my rant.*

It *feels like most women are shamed into*
responsibility, for men will be animals, it's their
ability they say. But then they go ladies are more
mature, it's a fact. Men can't control themselves,
that's the act, which is totally bullshit.

My *rant may be loud, but it's not lies, pure*
emotions and conflict.

Hypocrisy *and the patriarchy blinds you, while*
truth never dies.

Eve *nods in understanding.*

Thank *God I am not alive she says with a giggle.*

Girls are more mature.

You *know boys will be boys.*

What *did you expect Jeva men can't control*
themselves.

I *roar out lies, your hypocrisy tries blinding me*
but I don't eat where I shit like y'all.

Eve *is laughing at my fuming face turning into*
laughter.

The thirst

WHEN I WAS ONCE A HUMAN BEING

Do you enjoy being a ghost?

I'm not a ghost she states.

In some cultures or religious places I'm Saint she goes.

I wonder what the fuck that means.

I miss the ground under my feet Eve sighs out with bit of sadness.

What was it like, you know being alive?

She's getting flustered trying to remember Adam cuts her off

When I was once a human being, I roamed the earth with joy and glee. But then came Eve, my partner, I roll my eyes at this.

They holding each other tightly.

With a smile Adam continued.

Together we started life anew.

We laughed and loved and explored the land. Hand in hand, we made our stand. Once a human being, Eve was the best part of everything. She still is my everything he goes. I get more confused.

The thirst

MEXICAN APPLE SODA

In my childhood I'm told to behave
That I will one day I'll become someone's loving wife
It echoes throughout my head.
I'm now arguing with my mind as a young lady
Young adulthood is strange
I dream of a white dress and a veil, pink peonies,
I'm walking down the aisle feeling so frail.
Simple?
Right?
I'm scared of commitment I say to the therapist.
To be a bride is all I desire, I'm supposed to what
I'm told, my heart burns with an intense fire.
I'm go crazy I tell her
But as I wait for that special day, I sip on Mexican
Apple soda to bring hope and comfort, come what
may. Its sweet flavors and crisp tang, reminds me
that life is a colorful thing.
I'll keep dreaming of my wedding bells, and
savoring every sip of this sweet elixir that sells.
God, do you think I can it one day?

The thirst
APPLE BRANDY

Oh sweet Apple brandy, how divine, somebody
gonna die.
I hope it's not me tonight!
Oh, oh, oh I got soul
It feels lovely to be alive
With every sip, I feel so fine, wonder if ambrosia
taste like such.
Your flavor so complex and bold, leaves my taste
buds forever sold, I go breathless.
I'm my own champion in my own right!
To enjoy you is pure delight, expect no freight or
fight.
A pleasure to savor every night, only allow myself to
drink at times, and oh I feel it in my soul.
Your aroma, so sweet, and heady.
Makes me feel like a saved fool at last.
I toast to your brand, oh Apple dear, can't get
enough. For bringing me nothing but cheer. I feel
dazzle by the fact.
With each sip, I offer my praise. For you are the
true star of my days.

TEMPTATION

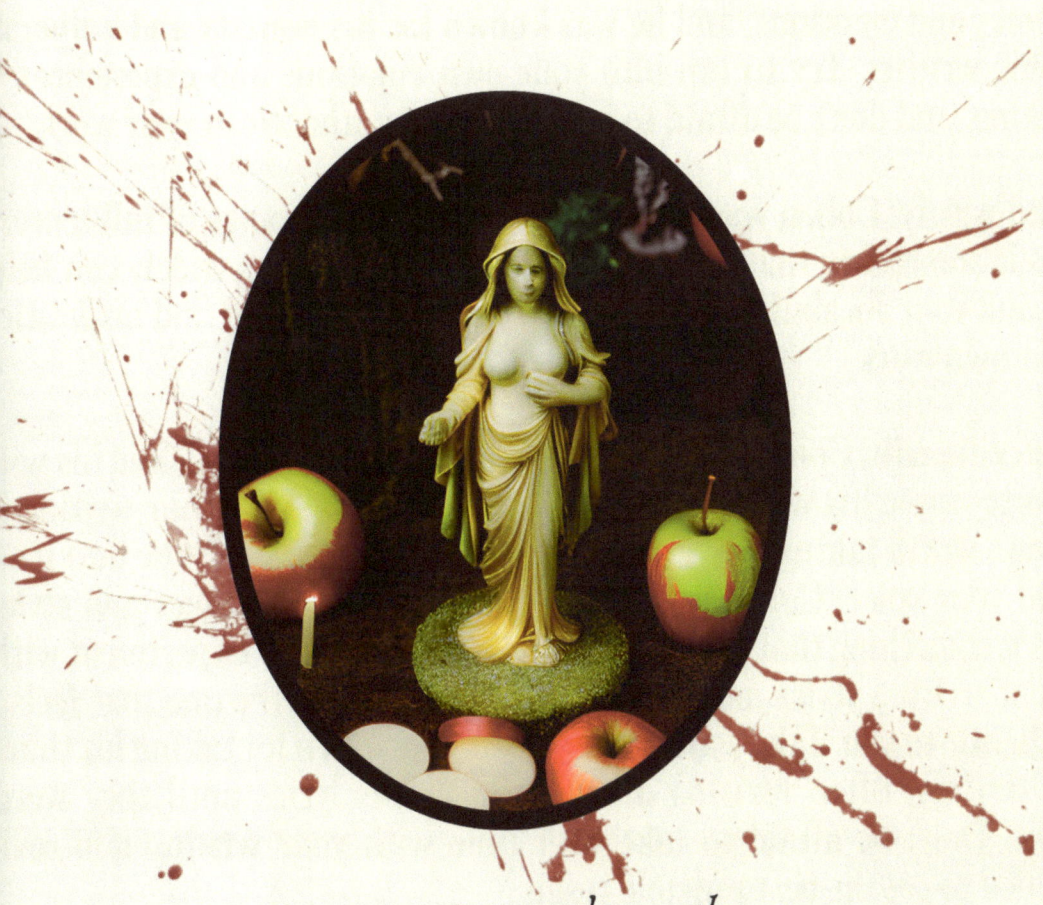

I crave it I say with a smile
She laughs for awhile
Don't we all?

SIN OF BEING A WOMAN

Eve, *did you enjoy your first time?*
No, *no, I suppose well I'm supposed to tell you no. But at*
the beginning it was lovely and Adam was tender with
me with everything afraid of breaking me I supposed.
There was a spot near the gardens with waterfall with
sandy white floor with plush leaves like a rainforest.
That's where he had me before we both know of pain
was.
Eve, so you enjoyed having sex?
She's blushing red as she can
She whispering out no like a lie
I go it's okay if you did or didn't
Eve stutters out softly it's sin of being a woman, were
supposed not be so human with expectation to be more
righteous and giving until we die out cold and bitter
Eve *looks ill saying* I seen what have others said we're
supposed be frigidity dolls of pleasure or mother to all,
pretty sad the newer generations are failures of stopping
falling in our footsteps again

THE TEMPTRESS

I'm the golden embrace, pleasure on
someone's tongue, and a reminder of fun.

They call me...

I just smile and flutter my eyelashes like
a fool

Oh, honey, I'm going to break your heart
if you're not careful

Yet, they hardly listen or not realize I
know they only see me as my body

WHORE RED

Red is the color of whores

I supposed so?

It can be bringing in the passion leading
weak men out to sea, getting themselves
worked up now, and I go that's fucking
pathetic.

Red is friend or an evil for some

But for me it's a delight or treat that
paints me kindly

so I guess I'm just another whore as well
I grow knowing smile that turns into a
smirk as I start to giggle at my own joke

SINS ON MY BREATH

My man's name lives under my breath

Eve is not amused by my behavior

He's mine I go

She scoffs out he isn't even your
husband!

I roll my eyes

Eve softly whispering He will hurt your
heart again, please let this one go for
good this time

My greatest sin was saying your name
and believing you ever be mine
Eve was right about you

UNDER THEIR EYES

Why are they watching us?

I sigh out sadly Men tend to stare at us
like prey and they declare themselves the
hunters

Eve questioning, You meant to say
predators?
No

Now I'm running just incase as for Eve
worriedly watches

Do they tend to chase after some of you
ladies?

I nod quickly thinking please don't let
him kill me

Temptation

DEVIL'S LIES ON HIS BREATH

He *calls* himself the Devil
I *laugh* because the boy's given government name
is a Bible name
I *should've* known better

When man says he's the devil trust him
Run, run, the *fuck* out of there fast!
Those are red sirens warning you the worst yet to
come

No *matter* how charming he is, or beautiful, and
loving he is now
He's *lying,* it's a trap, and don't look back
For *that* man speaks in the devil's native tongues

Be *free*
Run

TO BE A APPLE STRUDEL

To be an apple strudel, let's pretend!
Golden brown, be fresh, and sweet.
Layers upon layers of pastry, a treat for all to eat,
don't let consume you all.
To be a proper lady, poised, and full of grace.
I must have a pretty face as well.
Manners, style, and etiquette, in every social
space.
Two very different things, yet both so divine,
how can I dive into being satisfied?
When will I be happy?
One for the taste buds, the other to shush others
rude tongues towards my family name, the other
for the mind.
To be both at once, a challenge indeed, and great
challenge for me, imdeed. But to master both, I
hope to succeed.
Is a feat to exceed.

CARAMEL APPLE CHEESECAKE

*In the fall, the air grows cool, and my sweet tooth
starts to show through.
I began to drool.
Life can be cruel.
For a caramel apple cheesecake slice, I'll gladly
pay any price. I must wait until I earn it so.
But oh, the temptation that it brings, oh I can
hardly wait, my cravings soar on caramel wings.
I know I shouldn't indulge so much, but the taste
is just too rich to touch.
I fear this is only what I crave for
So I give in to the sweet desire, and savor each
bite like it's a fire. Temptation may lead me
astray, forgive me father.
Holy father look away for may I get to eat
without judgement of having pleasures.
But with caramel apple cheesecake, I'll be okay.*

WAS IT AN APPLE?

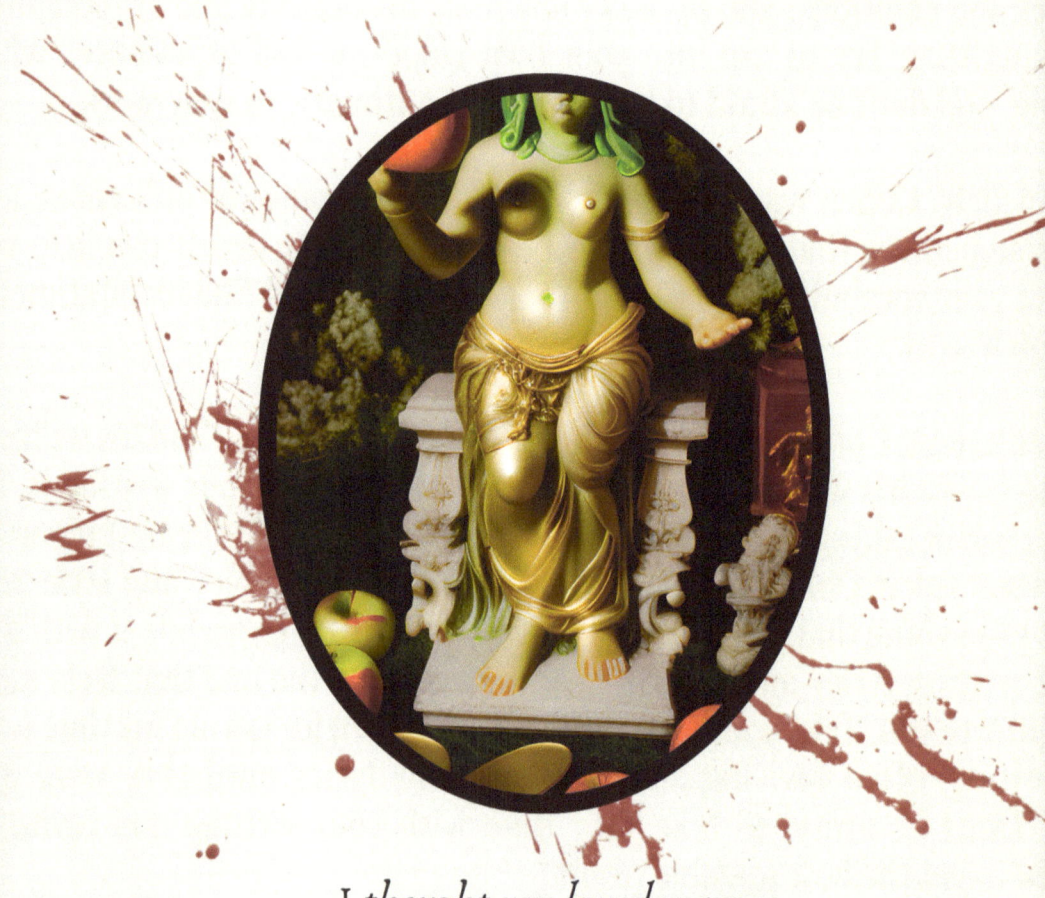

I *thought you loved mangos*
I *do, but* I *enjoy red fruits too*
Like?
Strawberries, Cherries, *and stuff like that*
What *about apples?*
I *enjoy the sour green ones actually*

Was it an Apple?

BIG BROTHER ALWAYS KNOWS

Eve giggled out the question why must
you call some men bitches?
I *laugh out, they feared to be feminine or*
compared to opposite biological sex due
seemingly means they lack powe, lack
dick and balls, just female dog in chains
But don't you get scared what might do
to you?

Duh, Eve they're always watching most
us anyways, or forcing themselves into a
place that didn't ask for their
experience, and then playing victim when
someone treats them the same way

Eve is panicking
I *just shrug, Welcome to modern world*
Eve, we're totally fucked

Was it an Apple?

THE PRICE OF KNOWLEDGE

Why did you do to get that?
Get what, Eve?
Your knowledge, there's no single
forbidden fruits on your table

I go hesitatingly, I used read books you
see, I went to early college high school
program, then force myself to university.
It took a lot out me, I cried more than I
enjoyed it honestly.
No, that's not what I meant.
Oh, what did you mean then, Eve?
Why do you know how to be and connect
to me?

I don't know what you mean by that.
I was born with it, I guess
But everything has a price because now
many call me crazy

Was it an Apple?

THE SINNER, THE HYPOCRITE, AND THE ZEALOT

Eve?
Eve huffs out of anger rolling her eyes, they are at it again!

The sinner is laughing at them, the hypocrite is getting red fuming at the mouth, and the zealot is screaming. They argued with Eve again, I sigh only watching them, their beliefs in a knot.
Was the forbidden fruit an apple, they asked.
Eve grows frustrated.
I try cut in, screams become louder.
Or perhaps a fig, a pomegranate unmasked? Maybe a fucking raspberry!? Shut up, sinner! In the end, it mattered not what it was, for their obsession with the fruit caused a fuss.
They forgot the lesson, the true moral, and instead focused on a mere detail. Eve leaves and so do I. That in their blindness, they failed to see, the true meaning of the forbidden tree.

Was it an Apple?

ONLY HYPOCRITES JUDGE EVE

Do you regret it?

Or of course not!

Eve's face turn sour as the hypocrite grows an awful smile

Eve and hypocrites end up in debate.

Somehow I'm their referee.

Her actions they love to berate.

She's screeching out,but do they practice what they preach? Their own flaws they fail to teach!

Hypocrites laughing thinking it's a win.

Pointing fingers with self-righteous pride! Hypocrites, their own sins they hide.

They grow red fuming at the mouth at Eve.

Eve stands strong, defends her choice.

I giggle believing hypocrites are pathetic, which says a lot about me.

While they mask their own inner voices.

So let us not judge, lest we be judged. For hypocrisy will leave us smudged. Let us instead seek truth and love And rise above the fray, like a dove.

Was it an Apple?

WE COULD'VE BEEN SISTERS

Welcome!
Here today, I have Lilith and Eve with me to talk about rumors
about themselves.
So, ladies who wants to go first?
The air grows tense
I'm slowly sweating
Lilith and Eve, oh what a pair, cracks a joke from Lilith's mouth.
Softly giggling out Eve says, sisters we could've been, if life was
fair.
Both created from the same divine hand. They let go some
bittersweet laughter. Yet, their stories couldn't be more different or
grand.
They chat out slowly as they seem to be afraid of another.
Lilith, the rebel, refused to submit, to Adam's dominance, she
wouldn't quit it. Cast out and demonized, she found her own path,
and now a symbol of freedom, she still inspires wrath.
They could been unstoppable I think to myself.
Eve, the first wife, the mother of all, her choice in the garden led to
humanity's fall. But through her pain, redemption was born. A
symbol of love, she continues to adorn.
Sisters in spirit, if not in name, Lilith and Eve, forever intertwined
in fame.
Let their stories not repeat again

I, THE DAUGHTER AM THE BETRAYAL

They wanted another son, Eve!

Eve shakes her head as a no

I sigh in conflict

I roughly cry out

I, the daughter, am the betrayal, I'm the wrought of guilt and shame. Eve comes to comfort me, to ease my troubled pain.

My tears try to drown me.

She reminds me of her own fall, from grace and pure delight. But through forgiveness and love, she explains now I must find my path to light.

I'm choking slightly gasping for help.

So I take solace in her words, slowly growing tired in myself, and listen to the hope they bring to me. For even in my darkest hour, I shouldn't doubt myself.

There is a chance to be set free.

BAKED APPLES

Baked apples and love spells, what's the difference
y'all? A magical combination that excels. Let me put
you under my spell?!
A treat for both heart and soul, warmth for the
soul, that can make any heart whole.
As the apples bake in the heat, I follow through
with a happy beat, love spells are cast oh so sweet.
Can I put a spell on you?
Aromas of cinnamon and spice, entice and warm like
a lover's embrace, I crave safety and romance.
Oh, oh, my
Everything that shines doesn't make it gold.
So let us savor this divine creation, of our happy
creattions, and let's eat happily.
And let's indulge in love's sweet temptation.
Make some baked apples for a lover which happens
to you

Was it an Apple?

APPLES IN WITCHCRAFT

In ancient times, apples are associated with
goddesses of fertility and love.
Golden apple caused a grand scandal back in
ancient days.
In Norse mythology, apples were believed to provide
eternal youth and were given as gifts to the gods.
Imagine the altars filled plenty of apples during
those days.
In medieval Europe, apples were used in divination,
with the direction of the apple peel indicating the
first letter of a future spouse's name.
Makes me wonder who's will be my future lover?
In the infamous Salem witch trials, an accused
witch was said to have used an apple to cast a spell
on a young girl.
We weep at violence, many witches that were lost,
and we learn to not repeat again.
Today, apples are still a popular ingredient in
modern-day witchcraft, with their symbolism often
associated with love, abundance, and knowledge.

FORBIDDEN FRUITS FOR GOOD GIRLS

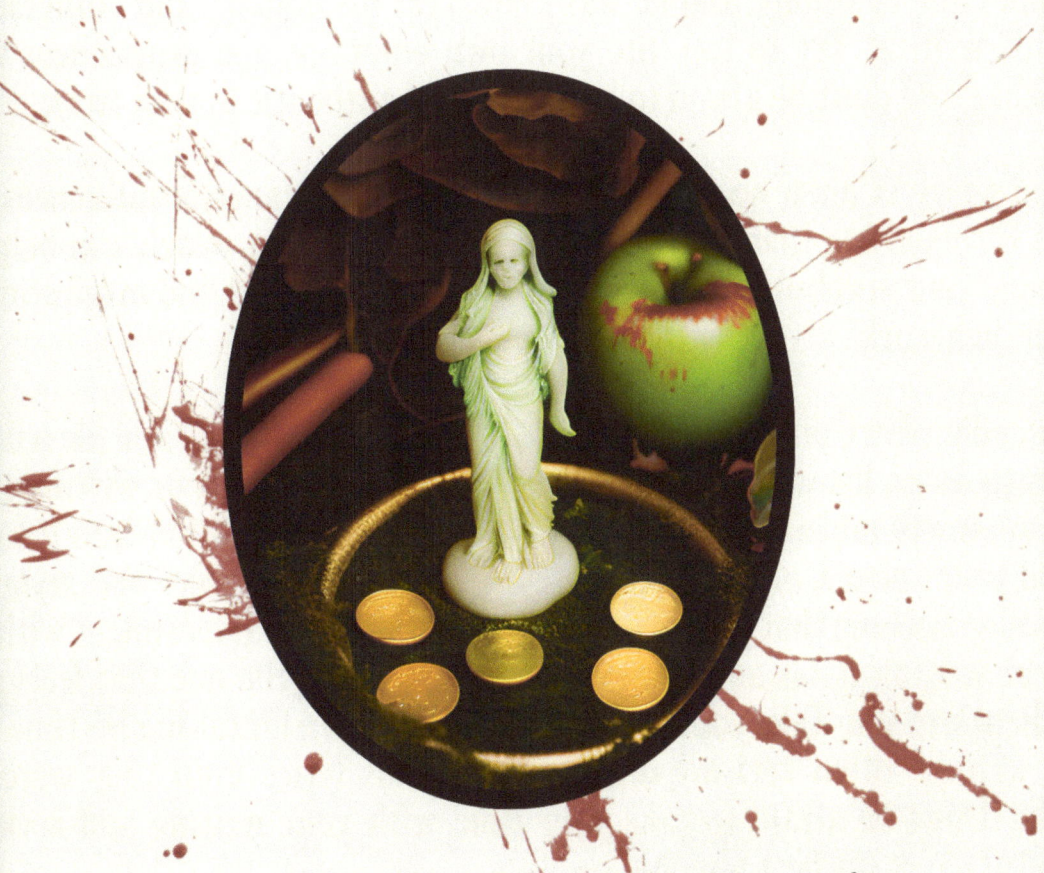

Jeva, you know what happens on wedding night?
We don't need have this talk
Google taught me about consensual honeymoon sex is,
mother!

THE FALL OF EVE

Was it like a mango?
Juicy
Full of life
Making you sticky in the end?!
No.
Eve began to remember
In the garden of Eden, Eve stood tall, conflicted at
hand.
With fruit so tempting, she couldn't resist at all. She
stared at it as the chaos began.
Was it like a mango, juicy and sweet, or an apple so Red
very ripe?
She licked her lips reaching out
Full of life, and oh so neat? But once she tasted, the
end was nigh, and everything grew cold. Sticky with
knowledge, she couldn't deny.
It was more than one fruit, silly she laughs out!
I'm afraid of asking her again

ALL OF EVE

You miss anything?

I miss my curls of my hair, braiding my girls hair,

and I miss making art.

I miss life that once was like my dear babes rosy

cheeks and growing smiles.

I liked taken charge of everything that I owned even

others try questioning me.

I didn't care about them.

I miss the gardens of Eden and the other versions of

us.

What!?

Eve grows red rushly explaining I said too much.

I was more than body, women, and mother.

I was human and still found happiness

WHY, ADAM?

Why him?
Why not?
*There were others, same names but different versions
of it, yet we end up together.*
Did you choose him or?
*Oh, of course I chose him silly child, who else was
supposed give him the privilege to breath in my same
air.*
Oh, I didn't mean to offend you my dear Eve.
So, why this Adam?
*He was the first give me those pink Hawaiian flowers
and often didn't mind to walk me to the ocean. He
was more into gathering with me, never jealous that I
liked to talk. He's tan skin reminds me golden sun's
rays.*
Oh, do tell!
No, smiles Eve with a wink

THAT'S WHAT HELL IS WISHING FOR

Get a grip child!
I'm in my depths of despair again, I'm trying not
to cry, Eve is yelling at me as well. When all
seems lost and bare, we may find ourselves there,
sit in it. Wishing for a way out of the nightmare.
But beware, my friends, our minds can play tricks
on us.
For sometimes what we wish for ends up being
worse than what we had. This might be a battle
but it's not the end of war. A new kind of hell
that makes us sad.
I cry
Eve tires to mother me from the unknown
But fear not, for Eve is here, and things unknown
who are willing to help you through life. With her
wise words to calm our fear, she reminds us to
keep pushing through, and find the strength to
start anew.

THEY CLAIMED AS THE ANTICHRIST

Eve is trying to comfort me
I'm evil
No, you're just completely different.
I feel cold
Eve is tired seeing be crying or somewhat dying
My breath grows shallow
Will I ever be the best?
Will I just be enough for anyone?
Eve sighs you're asking the wrong questions, my
dear!
I let her humming put to sleep once again
Eve knows I'm trying
But I lose myself when they call the devil's
daughter
It always ends the same I'm crying in pain

FORGIVE THEM FATHER, THEY'RE FROM RECKLESS FATHERS

DISGUST

They take without asking

PAIN

They use brutality as the only action

PITY

They haven't weep since they were newborns

SORROW

I dance in those mixed emotions
Forgive them father, for they know not what they do I
think to myself
As my body is overflowing
Born of reckless fathers, they struggle to break through
I *whisper*
Raised with broken hearts, believing violence God given
right, and shattered dreams to bear. They are unholy and
unhappy spreading it to new bloodlines each day. Feel
them watching as I dance and sing. They stumble through
life, with burdens hard to bear, but still they carry on.
With hope that one day they'll find A way to break the
cycle, and leave the past behind.
Yet, some reason some of them try to kill us all.
So forgive them father, and guide them through the
strife, or simply destroy us all. Help them find
redemption, and a better way of life. Or step aside watch
me kill those who try taking advantage of me as I dance
along.

CIDER AND THE ORIGINAL SIN

With a hidden orchard full of life, I found my delight, please don't grow to fight me?
Amongst the apples, red, and oh, so bright.
The crisp breeze rustled through the trees, I hear the birds singing, are your ears ringing?
As I sipped on cider, sweet, and pleased.
With each sip, I felt the sin, oh, no I feel the thrill!
Of pleasure and joy, deep within. The original taste, pure and true, who ever knew?
A moment of bliss, just me and you.
So let us raise a glass and cheer, let's love and laugh at last!
To the simple joys that bring us near. To cider, pleasure, and original sin, I feel my growing grin.
A moment of peace, let us revel in.

EVE'S APPLE CIDER DELIGHT

Eve's Apple Cider Delight,
A recipe that's sure to excite. Start with fresh apples, crisp and sweet, then simmer them down to a perfect treat.

Add some cinnamon and a touch of spice, And let the flavors meld together nice. Pour in some cider, let it all stew, and soon you'll have a drink that's fresh and new.

Garnish with an apple slice or two, And enjoy this tasty drink, it's good for you. Eve's Apple Cider Delight, A recipe that's sure to take flight.

Here's a liquor inspired drink based off the Eve's Apple Cider Delight

Eve's Apple Cider Delight can be made by mixing apple cider, spiced rum, and a splash of triple sec. Add a cinnamon stick for garnish and serve over ice. For a non-alcoholic version, replace the spiced rum with ginger ale or apple juice. Enjoy the sweet and tangy flavors of this delicious fall-inspired drink.

APPLE CIDER, PLEASE?

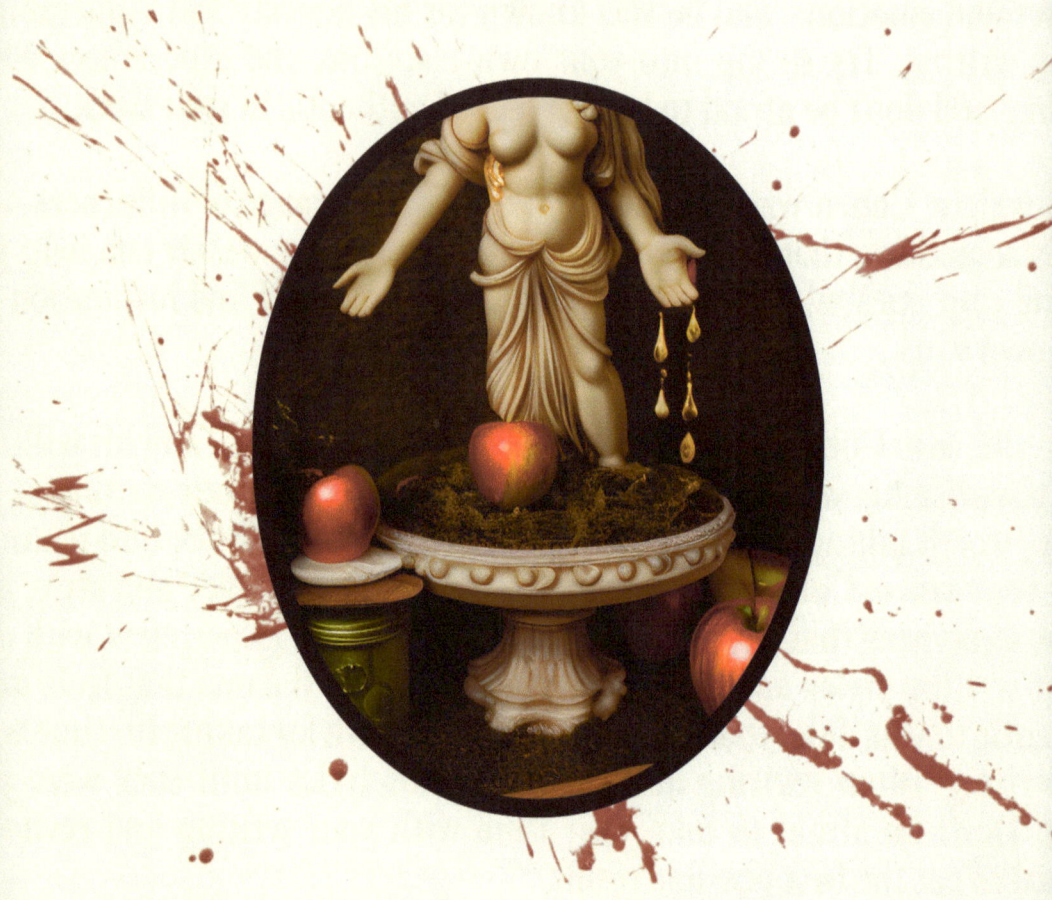

Really want it so bad.
You got wait until marriage!
I was talking about apple cider, Mamá!?

Apple cider, please?

A TASTE OF SIN

Is *like a red candy apple with dipped in*
chamoy and a kick of spice.
Mouthwatering
Delicate as it seems
A process to complete
It's a flavor so tempting, it's almost
sinful, a treat that leaves your taste
buds tingling and grateful.
It can't be beat!
I can't to take a big bite out of one!
Apple juice down my tongue
Harsh candy on my mouth
I can't get enough
Better than bedding any man any day

Apple cider, please?

TO BE LIKE APPLE CIDER

Hot

I want to be hot

Maybe not?

Oh, how sweet you are, like apple cider, to be fair like such.

Your presence fills the room, a warmth beyond compare, I grow into desperation. Your charm, wit, and grace, a sight to behold!

To become my beloved to hold.

A true gem in a world that can be so cold.

To be careful in from their cruelty.

Like the finest blend, you are a delight, and can't refuse a drink!

A sip of your essence, and all feels right. Do you understand? May your flavor never fade, may your sweetness never wane, and I never want say your name in vain. For you are a treasure, like apple cider's reign.

I might even be in love with you

Apple cider, please?

APPLE CORE

I'm sucking on a apple core
I
I hope I choke on it
It's the bittersweetness of an end
CHEWING
Chewing on an apple core spitting out the seeds
Mamá says not be like that be a lady instead
Biting
I bite on a apple core then I chuck the damn
thing at his head
I miss it instead
He looks angry
His spit our murderous rage at my face
I only form a knowing smile
I bite into another apple
This time it's green
He looks red like some of the apple core threw at
him, I go oh well spit out my bitten apple at him
then run out of there
I think I should hit with my sour apple instead

Apple cider, please?

EAT UNTIL YOU REACH MY APPLE CORE

Created trust, rush of youth, and growing affection.

Lust shared

Heated stares

I'm aware he is undressing me with those damn eyes

His named after a an archangel

I wonder how he feels against my mouth

I want him sweating

I want him so bad

Eat until you reach my apple core, I whisper

He is grunting out roughly, for your hunger can never be satisfied.

I'm flustered his breath is against my ear as he takes charge

Your appetite for life and love is insatiable, I moan out a bit defeated. He's holding me dearly, he is laughing out, I am captivated by your every desire.

I give him a heated kiss

He smugly reciprocating back

Your bright smile is as sweet as a ripe apple, I giggle at his charm. I flutter my eyelashes at him, he's grinning at my thigh. And your eyes sparkle like the morning dew, I cannot resist your charm, and your grace. I shuttered at his words and kisses. For you are a beauty that stands out in any place.

Apple cider, please?

APPLE, SWEET POTATO, OR CREAM PIE?

Cream pie?
I *never made one before I go*
He *laughed like if I said a joke*
Slowly *he realizes I'm being honest*
I *can make an apple pie or sweet potato*
one, *instead?*
Eve *whispers in my head*
Sex, *he asking*
It *clicks in my head*
I *go oh*

He's *practically begging for his end*
Then *giggle out you're very desperate, so*
no *thanks*
I *start going into hiding before anything*
else *can happen*

Apple cider, please?

APPLE CINNAMON GOODNESS

Cinnamon hold power
Witches know best
I'm trying not be desperate eat it
everyday
Oh, to be soft, smooth, and unafraid
A sweet aroma fills the air, my stomach
hurts with growing hunger, a little treat
I say.
Apples and cinnamon, a perfect pair.
Can't wait to chew on and celebrate
A warm and cozy feeling inside, with
every bite, pure joy to abide.
A bit of sea salt and peanut butter for a
good life.
A dessert so simple, yet so divine!
Apple cinnamon goodness, oh how I pine.

Apple cider, please?

HOPE YOU CHOKE ON APPLE SEEDS

Frustration
I feel icky all the same
Biting with my teeth
My tongue licking raw
Apple juice began to fall
Dipping down my neck
Hope is a seed we plant in the ground, Nourished by patience, love, and sound. It grows and blossoms, strong and true, Bringing joy to me and you.
But like an apple, hope has seeds, which I hope you choke on!
Small and bitter, just like needs, don't lost your in bitterness. We must discard them, let them go, and let our hope and love then flow. As I left go of my own anger.
So, if you dislike apple seeds, remember hope is what we need. Plant it deep, let it grow, watch it flourish, don't you know?

Apple cider, please?

CREAM OF APPLE AND VANILLA

Beauty

Is subjective

Its fleeting like a human life

In the orchard's beauty, I see a sight to behold, I
might even laugh.

Cream of apple and vanilla, aroma that cannot
be sold, we're a slight to behold!

Soft petals dance in the breeze, I began to crave
juice of a peach or of apples soon, as the apples
sway on the trees. Sweetness that fills the air, the
beauty of nature, and so fair

Cream of apple and vanilla

Creamy, dreamy, and divine.

I want be such as that

A taste that's simply sublime. I dress myself in
lotion of scents of pie, cream of apple, and
vanilla.

Inspiring a poem of beauty, I crave to be such as
that as well. In this moment, I am truly happy.

Apple cider, please?

CREAM OF EVE

Beauty
Eve holds beauty in her soul
Her heart beats wildly
She is free
In the garden of Eden, where Eve once
roamed free, she felt everything.
A beauty so pure, as far as the eye could
see, and innocence to be.
She sways dancing with the trees.
With skin as smooth, as the cream of
apple and vanilla, sweetness nectar of
honey. Her beauty shone bright, even if
her heart as fallen, a sight that could
thrill ya.
Oh,oh, to be Eve
Oh, goodness, forgive me Eve, please?
Her grace and charm, dance of power,
were unmatched by any other!
A true work of art, a sight to discover,
the true mother.

TO BE A STUPID RED CANDIED-APPLE

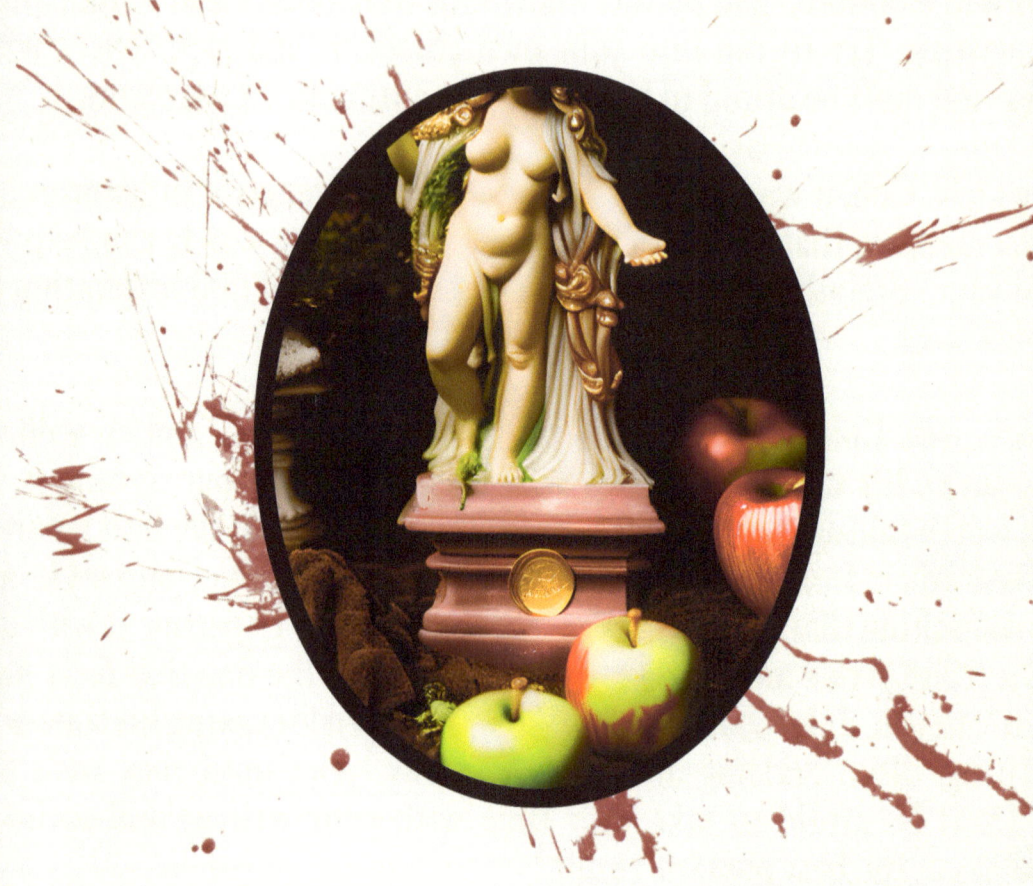

I hear the echoes of Eve in my mind, as a young lady, I was drawn to the red candied-apple like a moth to a flame, unaware of the consequences that would follow.

Fuck!

So, I use music and magic fix it instead

TO BE A DUMB VIRGIN

A insult

To be a dumb virgin.

Is to be pure and true?

But insults may come, and hurtful words too.

Pain try to dwell in our cells.

We must let go, let heal hopefully, today?

To deal with such offenses, can't not stay tall if y'all
are pinning me down, we can't get it let out with
violence?

One must have inner strength, remember their worth,
and all the good they bring!

For being true to oneself, is more important than any
jibe, those who insult and mock, pathetic vibe.

Are the ones with the real strife.

So mock me, for my soul shall set the stones of
protection or the hexes to honor my own.

To be a stupid Red Candied–Apple

GOING BLONDE

Going blonde, a change so bright, wanna
catch the sunlight in my highlights.
A transformation that's quite a sight!
Can't wait to catch my own eyes!
But with it comes a judgmental crowd
Whispers and stares, oh so loud!
Oh, lord!
But why must we conform to the norm?
Why not be different, break the form?
I'm young and I want to explore.
Even if I lose my youth I want try
Let's embrace our uniqueness, our flair
And show the world just how much we
dare
So dye your hair, go blonde with pride
Let the others talk, let them chide
For in the end, it's your life to live and
being true to yourself, what a gift.

To be a stupid Red Candied-Apple

STICKY

Sticky like homemade Apple Cinnamon Vanilla
Caramel Ice Cream.
A delicious dessert that combines the sweetness of
apples with the warm spice of cinnamon and the
richness of caramel.
A treat for the gods!? Or for all of us.
To make this ice cream, start by cooking diced apples
with cinnamon and sugar until they are soft and sticky.
Then, mix in a vanilla ice cream base and stir in a
generous amount of caramel sauce.
Like a magical spell in a pot!?
Freeze the mixture until it is firm, and serve with a
drizzle of additional caramel sauce and a sprinkle of
cinnamon on top. Your guests will love this unique and
indulgent ice cream!
This spell of comfort and to succeed of relaxing!
Please enjoy it safely!

To be a stupid Red Candied-Apple

HOMEMADE STICKY

Ingredients:

2 cups heavy cream

1 cup whole milk

3/4 cup granulated sugar

1 teaspoon ground cinnamon

1/2 teaspoon vanilla extract

1/2 cup caramel sauce

1/2 cup applesauce

1/4 teaspoon salt

Instructions:

In a saucepan, combine the heavy cream, whole milk, granulated sugar, ground cinnamon, vanilla extract, and salt. Heat over medium heat, stirring occasionally, until the sugar has dissolved and the mixture is hot but not boiling.

Remove the mixture from the heat and whisk in the caramel sauce and applesauce until well combined.

Transfer the mixture to a container and refrigerate until chilled.

Churn the mixture in an ice cream maker according to the manufacturer's instructions.

Transfer the ice cream to a container and freeze until firm.

This ice cream should have a slightly sticky texture due to the caramel and applesauce. Enjoy!

To be a stupid Red Candied-Apple

THE APPLE OF MY EYE

"Do not give dogs what is sacred; do not throw your pearls to pigs. If you do, they may trample them under their feet, and turn and tear you to pieces."
Used this carefully
Ingredients:
2 oz apple cider
1 oz mango juice
1 1/2 oz vodka
1/2 oz triple sec
Splash of lime juice

Apple slice and mango slice for garnish
Instructions:
Fill a cocktail shaker with ice.
Add apple cider, mango juice, vodka, triple sec, and lime juice.
Shake well until combined.
Strain into a glass filled with ice.
Garnish with apple and mango slice.
Enjoy your delicious "The Apple of My Eye with Mango" cocktail!

To be a stupid Red Candied-Apple

CIDER IN EDEN

Is *made with vanilla ice cream is a delicious and unique drink that is sure to impress.*

Must do a quick prayer for health.

Have mercy upon me, O LORD; for I am weak: O LORD, heal me; for my bones are vexed.

Or say positive things of your health.

To make it, start by adding a scoop of vanilla ice cream to a glass. Pour in a shot of apple cider and top it off with sparkling cider.

Stir gently to combine all the flavors. For an extra touch of sweetness, you can garnish the drink with a sprinkle of cinnamon or a drizzle of caramel syrup. Enjoy your Cider in Eden with vanilla ice cream and savor the rich, indulgent flavors.

To be a stupid Red Candied-Apple

THY APPLE?

*Thy Apple
His eyes are on my thighs
I want to covered my legs possibly hide
myself
Thy apple, red and ripe,
Tempting as it may be, is not an
invitation, to sexualize me.
Leave me alone!
I am not just a fruit, to be plucked, and
consumed!
I'm not a object for your choosing!
My worth is beyond my curves, stop
trying to eat me with your eyes, and
should not be assumed.
So let us celebrate, the sweetness of this
fruit, and see beyond its skin, to the
person it can suit.*

To be a stupid Red Candied-Apple

MORE APPLE JUICE?

More apple juice, Oh, how it soothes.
Supposedly it's only for a child.
But I never listened.
EVE SMILES FROM THE
HEAVENS

A sip, a gulp, I want to chug it down.
My thirst it busts.
I DON'T CARE IF I BRING YOU
HELL
Being comfortable, in my own skin, as a
young lady, is where I begin.

LET ME EXIST IN MY OWN SKIN

With each sip, I feel more at ease, I'm
allowed to find peace. Confident and
content, as I please.

To be a stupid Red Candied–Apple

SIPPING CIDER WITH EVE

Sipping cider with Eve, I asked about
her belief, and whisper like it's
confession.
In female intuition, a gift beyond our
cognition.
She looked at me dearly.
She spoke of a sixth sense, a power to
make sense Of the world around us,
And guide us with trust.
I listened with wonder, As she shared
her ponder On the mysteries of life,
And the wisdom of a wife.
Sipping cider with Eve, I learned to
perceive! The magic in a woman's
mind, And the treasure we can find.

To be a stupid Red Candied–Apple

FRESH APPLE PIE

"Being like a fresh apple pie, sweet, and warm, is a feeling that comes naturally when you know your worth and beauty. Embrace your inner confidence and let your radiance shine through like the delicious aroma of freshly baked pie."

Oh

Oh, oh baby I want to be his fresh baked pie

I might even let him put bun in my oven
Jeva, behave!?

Yet, without shame I drool look after him
I wonder if he would like eat vanilla ice cream on me too?

To be a stupid Red Candied–Apple

APPLE SAUCE

*"I scoop a spoonful of apple sauce and try
to eat it with ladylike poise, but secretly
I wish I could just dive into the jar and
devour it with reckless abandon."*

*She's mad and disappointed in me again
I cry*

*Eve sighs out worriedly "Your mother
just wants the best for you, understand?"*

*She asked for too much outta me whisper
in the darkest of bed and room*

TO BE LOVED LIKE APPLE FRITTERS

"To be loved like apple fritters - sweet, comforting, and always satisfying. But also craving healthy, passionate love - the kind that nourishes your soul and sets your heart on fire."

What the fuck is a Apple Fritter I scream in frustration
Eve rolls her eyes at me shushing me rudely

I blush researching my new curiosity
Oh
Oh, oh, to be beloved like damn apple fritters, do you think it's possible for me?
Eve giggles with a growing smile
You are most odd maiden ever watched over, yet!?

WITH LOVE

*To struggle is not a blessing, to suffer
never meant to be a gift, you are allowed
to want more and rest.*

I hope you have a best life

Fuck!

You are allowed to change and grow!